I0390641

The BIGGEST Bully & What YOU Need to Know

How to MAKE the IRS Behave!

Alissa K. Mennenga Hollinger, CPA, CTRS

ISBN-13: 978-1540439932
ISBN-10: 1540439933

DEDICATION

The IRS has ruined lives and a LOT of them with their bullish ways! To all those taxpayers who have been abused, I'm so very sorry! Therefore, I dedicate this book to ALL taxpayers who have to deal with the IRS.

CONTENTS

ACKNOWLEDGMENTS

To Scott: my crazy, fun loving husband, you have been with me since I started on this meandering journey of having my own firm. When we said I do, we only thought we understood the demands that tax season would bring. Each and every year, as the firm has grown, it has required more of my time. You have never complained about it, except maybe after April 15th, but I'm pretty sure that doesn't count. I could NEVER have done this without your support. By the way, I LOVE, LOVE, LOVE it when you do the dishes, laundry, vacuum, dust, and all the other things I struggle to get to at the end of the day.

To my mother: you have brought so much to the firm. I know that over the years the technology we have implemented has been extremely challenging, overwhelming, and intimidating. You have given me 200% and always willing to do anything I have asked. You may be one of the few people that truly understands my fear of those big nasty bugs, so THANK YOU for always being on guard!

To my son: I must be pretty amazing! Through all of this, I have managed to raise the most incredible young man! You're kind, intelligent, and a workaholic; pretty much another me ☺. You have been there from the first semester, thank goodness you don't remember sleeping in the library! There have been moments when you sincerely hated me and moments when you refuse to listen to me. But, in the end, we made it through and I hope you know I love you from the bottom of my heart!

To my sister-in-law Kimmy: when I offered you a position, I had no idea where that would lead us. However, you have become someone whom the thought of losing brings me nightmares and panic attacks. You are FORBIDDEN to ever leave me! Oh how I love you, my Pisces twin!

Last, to my little brother Robert (pretty sure he hates it when I call him little). Because of you, I am heading off in directions I would never have considered on my own. You have always believed in me and are the only person that may be as smart as I am ☺! I am so grateful to have you on my team and excited to see the amazing opportunities that await you. Together, we are unstoppable!

Alissa

1. IN THE BEGINNING

If you were to take a random poll asking folks what they thought about the Internal Revenue Service (IRS), I would bet money that it would be 95% negative. Now don't get too excited, the positive 5% may simply be that the IRS didn't take their home! The fear that I often see and hear, in terms of the IRS, is staggering. Why? Because the IRS is the BIGGEST bully in town!!!

The arms of the IRS seem to have no limits or boundaries, and unlimited resources available. They are everywhere and can touch everything! They have access to the largest databases of collected information at their disposal.

Think about it, they are the collection agency for the United States Government. The same Government that has the ability to impact entire nations with a military force respected, feared, and hated worldwide. The IRS has a job to do: collect money and enforce the rules! They are the money police!

However, like any bully, they can be made to behave, you just need to know how. That's what this book is about. I am tired of seeing taxpayers afraid to check their mail because of "nasty grams" from the IRS. I am sick and tired of hearing stories of good people afraid to go home or even open a bank account, because of the IRS. The IRS and the disjointed, tangled, mess of a tax system we are in can be overwhelming and incredibly frustrating, even for tax professionals.

If this book only helps one person realize there is hope and there ARE options, I will call this a roaring success.

How bad can it really be?

We all know that the IRS collects taxes. We also know that there are consequences for not dealing with certain aspects of our tax obligations. However, do you really know what the IRS is capable of? If you've never had a run-in with the IRS, some of these stories may shock you. I know that when I first started my tax career, I had no idea what kind of trouble was out there.

The IRS can take your money! That's right, they can take every single dollar from your bank account. When this happens, causing the mortgage payment to bounce or the debit card not work when it's time to pay for groceries, it's time to take notice. You have rights!

They can seize your assets! Yep, they can put a lock on the door and take your office building. Can you imagine being the owner of a struggling small business and when you arrive to start your day, you're not allowed in? What will your customers or employees think? This is devastating and can feel impossible to overcome. However impossible it may seem, you have rights!

They can, and will, dictate who you can and cannot pay. Talk about control freaks, they have standards to determine how much you can pay for rent or for food. They have stipulated how much you should be paying for clothing, utilities, transportation, etc. If it doesn't meet their definition of necessary and essential, not happening!

They can take your retirement account! That's right, they can take your IRA, 401(K) SIMPLE, SEP, and any other retirement plan you have scraped by to save. I don't think it's a surprise that our social security benefits are dwindling and the common belief that it will be gone when it's our time to collect. What are you supposed to do when you can no longer work and your miniscule social security benefits dry up? That's your problem to figure out because the IRS has their own problems to deal with.

Did I mention garnishing your wages? They can take up to 50% of your paycheck. We all know that most often 100% of the paycheck isn't enough OR you wouldn't have IRS problems! What are you supposed to do with even less? Again, that's your problem, not theirs!

I could go on and on but I think I've painted a pretty discouraging picture. I have had grown men in my office with a look of despair that literally brought me to tears. I have heard of neighbors committing suicide because of taxes and widows wondering how they were going to keep the business going.

Like with any bully you have to stand your ground. When dealing with the IRS, you MUST know your rights, your options, and have a game plan. I am a firm believer in understanding the rules and how you can play the game. I believe that knowledge is power and that the underdog can win! However, this is not our junior high battleground and the good ol' boy ways won't cut it!

Ever heard the saying history always has a way of repeating itself? Most of us recall the colonial protest against British taxation in the 1760's which led to the American Revolution.

The 13 colonies rejected the authority of the British Parliament to tax them. Say what? In fact, the British taxed the colonies to get out of debt and strictly enforced collections. Say what? Even worse, laws could be imposed on the American colonies without legal objection since the colonies had no representation in Parliament. As to be expected, soon Britain began to see the tax revenue as a nice and steady income source. I know, it's starting to sound very current if you ask me.

As you know, we won our independence in 1776 and now we have the 4th of July! It didn't stop there, in 1789 the United States Constitution became the supreme law of the United States of America.

Originally comprising of 7 articles, the Constitution has been amended 27 times. Our Constitution is an incredibly dynamic foundation and our founding fathers were very insightful.

But you're probably most interested in the amendment dealing with your taxes. The 16th amendment was submitted July 12, 1909 and was accepted February 3, 1913.

This was the beginning of history repeating itself all over again. Please don't misunderstand, I am not protesting taxes because I sincerely believe they are a necessary evil.

However, I do believe that taxes are seen now as a steady stream of income. Unlike the British, who used the money to actually pay off their debt, our country continues to create a significant amount of debt that is growing every day. Unfortunately, the collections are simply not enough to sustain our Government.

We are taxed when we earn the money, when we spend the money, and annually on many assets we've acquired with money that's already been taxed. Tax, tax, tax!!!

Like the British, the Internal Revenue Office has been known to strictly enforce the collection of taxes. I'm assuming that you or someone you know owes taxes that you simply can't pay. If so you are not alone.

Enough with the doomsday, let's get to the stuff you really care about, the stuff you need to know now!

2. DO YOU NEED A PROFESSIONAL?

A common question I hear is do you really need a professional? Well, like most situations, it depends on several different factors. However, 99.9% of the time I recommend it, just as I usually recommend a visit to the DR when you know it's more than a common cold. But, who can help you with this? Will you need a CPA, EA, or an attorney? They can all get the job done to one degree or another. For example, a heart doctor can treat strep throat but that's over kill when your family doctor will be more than adequate and definitely cheaper.

Under the Internal Revenue Code, Congress made it very clear who they felt would be qualified to represent people when dealing with the IRS. The entire list of professionals is narrowed down to three different designations.

1) A Certified Public Accountant (CPA)
2) An Enrolled Agent (EA)
3) An Attorney

CPAs are certified and licensed within each state by the state board of public accountancy. In addition, each state will have specific annual education and licensing requirements to meet. Although a CPA is allowed to provide most, if not all, accounting services some will chose to specialize in a few related areas. For example, I specialize in defending taxpayer rights, commonly referred to as tax resolution or tax relief.

EAs are enrolled agents licensed and regulated by the IRS. They may or may not have the same educational background as CPAs and they usually just focus on taxation. They also have annual education requirements mandated by the IRS but they may be less stringent than the annual requirements for CPAs. In the tax resolution world, CPAs & EAs tend to be equally qualified, at least when comparing credentials.

An attorney will usually have the least amount of a tax background, unless they are a tax attorney with a special degree in taxation. There are times when an attorney is needed but I prefer to handle as much without them, simply to try to keep the fees as reasonable as possible. We ALL know attorneys are expensive!

Now that you know who can represent you, keep in mind there are over 300,000 tax professionals licensed in the United States to deal with income taxation. Of the 300,000 less than 1% specialize in tax resolution. Even though there are many knowledgeable and quite skilled in tax preparation, tax resolution is a horse of a different color. Tax resolution has a different set of rules; most tax professionals prefer to stick to what they know, tax preparation. Unfortunately, there are more taxpayers who need representation than there are professionals able and willing to provide it!

3. SO, WHAT CAN THE IRS REALLY DO?

Now that you know who to look for let's talk about the collection process; what the IRS can REALLY do! It usually starts when you fail to file a tax return or have a balance due that you are unable to pay. Initially, the IRS will send a series of automated collection notices. Each will have a number and a slightly different measure of seriousness. However, if you receive letter 1058, head's up because it is the "real deal"!! This letter is the first opportunity you have to file a Collection Due Process appeal – and you should almost always do this. But, you ONLY have 30 days otherwise you may start giving up very important taxpayer rights! If you fail to do this, the IRS can actually seize your income and assets without ANY FURTHER NOTICE TO YOU!!!! There are other very serious letters to watch out for, however, be aware that without experience in this they all tend to look the same.

As the IRS moves through the series of letters, you may experience a variety of unpleasant methods of additional contact. Although the IRS has a variety of enforcement tools in their arsenal, two methods that are most often used to get your attention will be liens and levies.

A lien is one way the IRS notifies the public about your outstanding tax bill. In fact, a lien is public information showing the type and amount of tax that is owed. This is not exactly the kind of information that you want readily available. A lien encumbers, or "ties up" assets that you may own now and in the future. However, a lien by itself does not result in the physical seizure of your assets. In fact, I like to think of liens as the appetizer at dinner. It's just the beginning, and you KNOW there is more to come.

The other collection method is what I like to call the "snatch & run" method, commonly referred to as a levy. A levy, however, actually results in the LOSS of property or wages. The first is typically called a seizure and allows the IRS to physically take your assets – cars, boats, business equipment, houses, etc.

The second type of levy is more common. Here, the IRS is literally taking property held by a third party, typically a bank or employer. The IRS forces your bank to give them whatever is in your bank account at the time. It doesn't matter that you have outstanding checks that will now bounce. Can you imagine the stress and challenge of being left with 30-50% of your paycheck? What are you supposed to do now?

Now that you have an overview, let's look at liens and levies in more detail.

Liens

Once the IRS has determined that you owe taxes (called an assessment) they have 60 days to give you a written demand for payment. This is done through the series of letters I mentioned previously. If you don't pay the IRS – in full and within 30 days, a Federal Tax Lien automatically goes into effect. Some mistakenly do not realize that a lien attaches to what you currently own and ANY property that you WILL own in the future! If you owe less than $10,000, the lien will NOT be recorded in the official records and not made public. This is the "secret" lien. If you owe more than $10,000 the lien will be record or filed in the county you reside. Your tax problem is now public and common knowledge!!!

The primary problem with a recorded lien is that it becomes public record. That means it also becomes a part of your credit report. Many of my clients have impeccable credit apart from the tax lien. Unfortunately, the tax lien results in credit scores that are lower than someone who recently filed for bankruptcy. In addition, the tax lien now makes it almost impossible to buy or refinance a home or even borrow the money to settle with the IRS.

Hope is not lost, Congress has provided ways to minimize the impact of a lien on your credit and assets. You just have to understand your rights and the procedures, that's where we come in! One way to help if you're selling real estate is to receive a certificate of discharge from the IRS. There are very specific circumstances that will allow the IRS to issue this discharge.

Another option for a recorded lien may be subordination. Subordination lowers the priority of the tax lien relative to other liens. In most cases, a lender will not loan you money if the IRS has the first "priority" of all liens against the house. That will make it almost impossible to buy a house after a Lien has been recorded. It also makes it really difficult to refinance a house with a recorded lien. Fortunately, Congress recognized the challenge here and will allow the IRS to "subordinate" the lien, or allow the IRS to step back and let other liens take priority. Why would the IRS even consider this option? It may actually allow the IRS to receive payment for the taxes without actually seizing the home and trying to sell it.

The final way to address a recorded tax lien is to have the IRS actually withdraw the tax lien. This should be the ultimate goal of any tax resolution planning. However, the IRS will ONLY withdraw a tax lien if:

1) you pay the tax debt in full
2) you discharge the taxes in bankruptcy
3) you successfully complete an Offer in Compromise
4) the lien becomes unenforceable because of the statute of limitations
5) you owe less than $25,000 and you've entered into an installment payment plan.

A lien withdrawal is the ONLY way that you can get your credit back to where it was and provide freedom with your assets.

Bank Levy / Wage Garnishment

Seizure or levy, this is where the IRS actually takes your assets and/or income. They take what you have worked so hard for! The IRS uses seizures to take things that are in your possession. This could mean the vehicle you use to show your real estate clients, the truck you use to make a living, and the one you probably think is safe, your primary residence. If you have received a Notice of Levy from the IRS, you need to contact a tax professional immediately!!

Another type of levy is commonly referred to as a "garnishment". The IRS uses this collection method much more often than a seizure. With a garnishment/levy action, the IRS is attempting to take the asset from a 3rd party such as the bank or your employer. This is where it really hurts and they do it to get your attention. They must send notice of intent to levy, giving you an opportunity to start communications.

Remember the "snatch & run"? A bank levy is when the bank is forced to turn over the balance in your account. The bank must comply or face sanctions from the IRS. This levy is a one-time hit by the IRS and the bank must hold the funds for 21 days. After that, they must release the funds to the IRS.

The bad news, any checks that come in will not be honored by the bank unless additional money is deposited. Fortunately, the bank is required to hold the funds for 21 days before turning it over to the IRS. This is intended to allow you time to work out a solution with the IRS and possibly get some of your money back. It is vital that you contact your resolution specialist (Me for example) once you receive notice of the levy.

However, a bank account levy should never happen. When you receive the Notice of Intent to Levy from the IRS, you have 30 days to hire a resolution specialist (Me again) to start working and negotiating out a solution.

But, what if you don't have a bank account, think you're safe? Not so fast, the IRS can also levy (garnish) your wages. The IRS can also force your employer to withholding a percentage of your wages. Depending on many factors, the IRS can actually take up to 70-80% of your pay. You already couldn't pay your taxes and now you can't even pay the light bill.

Unlike the bank account levy, which is one-time per notice, a wage levy is ongoing and continuous until the IRS tells the employer to stop withholding the money. In addition, your employer is required to begin withholding immediately once it receives the notice from the IRS or face sanctions.

As with bank account levies, a wage levy should never happen. When you receive Notice of Intent to Levy, remember, you have 30 days before the IRS attempts the garnish. You should have plenty of time to hire a resolution specialist (You guessed it, Me) to find a solution to your IRS problems.

The last type of levy or seizure can be on various financial assets that many believe are "off-limits" to the IRS. Most people assume the IRS can't seize their retirement accounts, social security income, or primary residence. However, this simply isn't true. Although federal & state laws often protect these assets from most creditors, the IRS is different. The IRS has the authority to seize these normally-protected assets and income to pay your taxes.

Fortunately, the IRS usually reserves this method for uncooperative taxpayers, and may even require a court order in the case of your primary residence. However, if this is you, I hope you can run fast. You need to run as fast as you can to a resolution specialist (I know, Me) because you have a serious problem!

These are just a few brief details on the variety of collection methods that the IRS has at their disposal. They will not go away, they will not stop, and it will not get better on its own. So – PLEASE – stop ignoring the problem and begin addressing it today. We CAN help you and there are options!!!

4. THE STAND-OFF, WHO FIRES FIRST!

As with most areas of the law, there are time limits that prevent things from running on forever. For the IRS, these time limits are called "Statutes of Limitations". They can work for you or against you, depending on your individual case.

The two main statutes that I'll cover will be the "Three-Year Statute for Assessment" and the "Ten-Year Statute for Collections". This is where the stand-off begins and it all starts with who makes the first draw.

Three-Year Statute for Assessment

The IRS has three years to "assess" a tax debt against you. This assessment is the official pronouncement that you owe a certain amount of debt, including penalties. The IRS is prevented from collecting a tax from you if it fails to assess the tax within the three-year statute.

However, the three-year statute can be extended to six years if, the tax return omits a "substantial" amount of gross income. The IRS defines "substantial" as 25% or more of the gross income reported on the tax return.

Here's where the stand-off begins. There is NO statute of limitations if you fail to file a return! That's right, if you don't file (or shoot first) the IRS have as long as they need to assess the tax and collect against you. There is also no statute of limitations if you file a fraudulent return with the intent to evade tax or if you attempt to defeat or evade tax.

One of the MOST IMPORTANT steps a taxpayer can take is to file a return. As in any stand-off, whoever shoots first often has the upper hand. As soon as you file, the three-year statute will start to run and you're back in the game!

Ten-Year Statute for Collections

This is the statute that most taxpayers have heard about. Once the IRS assesses the tax, they generally have ten years to collect from you. The IRS has an acronym for this statute: "CSED" or Collection Statute Expiration Date. Therefore, if you somehow make it through ten years of IRS collection actions, you're done. The IRS can no longer take any type of action against you. Surprisingly, this actually does happen. Keep in mind though, with available technology and the tools at their disposal, the IRS will get VERY aggressive within the last 2 years of the CSED.

But, what happens if you don't file? The CSED clock never starts ticking! In addition, there are a few things that can "stop the clock" actually extending the CSED beyond 10 years. This is known as "tolling" and I think of it as pushing the pause button. Anytime the IRS is prevented from enforcing any type of collection action for the tax, the ten-year statute will pause or "toll".

There are many actions that can extend the CSED and I've given you a very limited overview of the two most common statutes. Most importantly, I want you to understand that you must file a return, it is actually in your best interest to file. Because without filing, you begin giving up control of the situation and begin losing options. So, get ready to "shoot first" and take control!

5. FILE, FILE, FILE!!!

If you are required to file a tax return, the due date is April 15th of the year following the tax year. For example, the return for tax year 2016 will be due April 15, 2017. This date is statutory, or law of the land, and cannot be changed. However, it can be extended to October 15th if the proper forms are filed.

So, what happens when you don't file? Not filing a tax return is the worst thing a taxpayer can do for their overall situation. The penalties alone can add 50% to the total balance.

The penalty for failing to file (FTF) a return on time can be substantial! The penalty is currently 5% of the tax due – per month – up to a maximum of 25%. In just 5 months, the total FTF penalty will be 25% of the original balance that was due.

Even worse, you may actually have had a refund! If you don't file in time, you forfeit the refund, making a donation to the United States Treasury. Unfortunately, if you owe taxes, you will ALWAYS be expected to pay the balance due. It truly saddens me to see taxpayers lose their hard earned money because of the way our tax code is structured.

As if those reasons aren't enough to encourage you to file, the IRS may be kind enough to do it for you. This is when the IRS files a Substitute For Return or "SFR".

However, this is seldom a good thing. The IRS is not doing you a favor. When preparing the SFR, the IRS will use whatever income has been reported and then only give you one exemption and the worst filing status.

It's even worse if you are self-employed, because they will use all the income but not give you credit for any business expenses. As you can imagine, the taxes due on the SFR are significantly higher than if the correct information had been used to prepare the return.

Another VERY important reason to file is to ensure your right to discharge the tax debt in bankruptcy. I understand that bankruptcy is often the last path any individual wants to travel down, but at times, it is a viable option. And yes, you CAN bankrupt out of taxes. Not all taxes and there are very specific rules and types of taxes that apply but it can be done!

The MOST important reason to file, in my opinion, is to ensure your rights as a taxpayer. The IRS simply will not work with you to resolve your tax problem until you are in compliance. In fact, until you file, the IRS has all of the control and will call the shots. Regardless of the balance owed, I can't stress enough, FILE, FILE, FILE!!!

6. SO, WHAT CAN YOU DO?

You have options and I'm going to share with you some specific techniques that may resolve your tax debt. Please keep in mind, this is just an overview of the various techniques, and is not intended to be a do-it-yourself guide. I just want you to be aware so you will be an informed consumer. This can be your guide to help you ask informed questions when seeking out professional help.

1) Pay your taxes in full
2) Installment agreement – paying your tax debt over time
3) Currently not collectible
4) Offer in Compromise – Settling for less than you owe
5) Innocent spouse relief
6) Bankruptcy
7) Interest and penalty abatement

Pay Your Taxes in Full

Alright, this seems obvious and is always the best option. Finding a way to pay the IRS in full can save a substantial amount of money, even if creativity is needed to do so. In addition, paying in full is the quickest way to get the IRS to remove recorded liens.

Therefore, I encourage you to consider this option first, In fact, now would be a great time to ask a family member for a loan or refinance your home.

Installment Agreement

The installment agreement is probably the option used the most. An installment agreement may allow you to repay your debt over many years. How long and the amount of the monthly payment will depend on the amount of debt you owe, along with your income and expenses.

There are several different types of installment agreements and the qualifications for each. Just remember, the longer you take to pay the more you will pay overall.

Guaranteed Installment Agreement

If you owe less than $10,000, the IRS has a special installment agreement for you . It's called a Guaranteed Installment Agreement. Under this program, you're guaranteed as long as you meet the following requirements.

1) You must owe $10,000 or less in income taxes;
2) You have filed and paid all tax returns during the five tax years before the tax debt;
3) You can't pay the debt in full from liquid funds;
4) You must repay the debt in 36 months;
5) You must file and pay all tax returns during the installment agreement;
6) You must not have had an active installment agreement during the past five years.

If you meet the requirements above, you qualify for a guaranteed installment agreement.

Streamlined Installment Agreement

As part of the Fresh Start Initiative, the IRS recently increased the amount of qualifying tax debt from $25,000 to $50,000. The IRS also increased the repayment time from 5 years to 6 years. To qualify for this agreement, you must meet the following criteria:

1) You must owe $50,000 or less in ANY type of tax debt.
2) You must be able to fully repay the debt within 72 months or before the expiration of the CSED.
3) You must have filed all tax returns due to date.
4) You must file and pay all tax returns during the installment agreement.
5) If you owe between $25,000 and $50,000 you will be required to enter into a direct debit agreement; whereby the IRS will debit the payment directly from your bank account. You may also be required to provide some minimal financial information during the application process.

In my opinion, the best thing about this type of agreement is that you aren't generally required to provide financial information to the IRS to qualify. Yes, I realize that they can get just about any information they want on your financial status, but there's no need to hand it over on a silver platter.

Even if you don't need the full 72 months to repay, life gets in the way. Because of this, I always recommend the smallest payment possible.

There are no early pay-off penalties if you can or decide to pay off the debt before the 72 months. However, if life happens and you default because the payments are too high, the IRS may not be so cooperative the next time.

Regular Installment Agreement

If you don't qualify for a Guaranteed or Streamlined Installment Agreement, you will probably need to consider a Regular Installment Agreement.

There is no minimum or maximum amount of tax to qualify for this. They payment will be based upon your assets and ability to pay, as determined by the analysis of your financial position.

The IRS will require you to complete a personal financial statement, typically a Form 433, and may require that you complete a business financial statement as well if you own a business.

This is where I come in! My job is to minimize my client's assets and disposable income that the IRS will look at to determine the monthly payment.

Many of my clients assume that since they have little to no money left over at the end of the month, they should be allowed to pay whatever they can scrape up. However, the IRS doesn't look at expenses the same way that you or I would.

The IRS has developed very specific financial standards that they use to determine what your expenses should be based on the size of your household. Regardless of what you spend on groceries or a mortgage payment, the IRS may determine that the amount is unreasonable for your household size.

This means that the IRS may determine that you can, and should, pay more towards your debt than what you really can pay. At least when compared to your current expenses.

The IRS agents have some flexibility in allowing your actual expenses. However, I've had numerous occasions where the agent was simply being unreasonable and I had to escalate to the agent's manager.

As I've said many times already, you should seriously consider seeking out the help of a tax resolution specialist (Remember me?) to help you negotiate a workable and properly structured installment agreement with the IRS. I can generally get the payments to an affordable amount, even if the IRS guidelines don't provide an affordable option.

The deadlines for completing a regular installment agreement will be the CSED. If you aren't able to pay the tax in full before the CSED, it may make sense to consider a Partial Payment Installment Agreement. Let's look at that now.

Partial Payment Installment Agreement

If you're not able to pay the tax debt in full before the CSED (Remember, this is Collection Statute Expiration Date), the IRS may approve a Partial Payment Installment Agreement.

The IRS will want to verify that you truly don't have the ability to pay the debt in full before the CSED. In order to do this, they will require that you complete, document, and file a financial statement before it agrees to allow you to repay less than the full amount. They will also require that you sell or borrow against any assets that you have to pay down the debt.

Although this may be a good option for you, an Offer In Compromise may also be good. In fact, it may even be better!

The majority of taxpayers will utilize some type of installment agreement to resolve their tax debt.

Currently Not Collectible

Many taxpayers that have outstanding tax debt are struggling to just put food on the table. It is often impossible to make ANY payments to the IRS without sacrificing essential needs.

Fortunately, the IRS has a temporary solution for this and it's called Currently Not Collectible or CNC. Although the IRS actually has several reasons for placing a tax account in CNC status we are only going to address financial hardships.

CNC status will stop all IRS collection activity providing time for the taxpayer to get back on their feet. To qualify for this status, the IRS will generally require you to complete Form 433-A and/or Form 433-B. If the financial information you provide indicates you have no or few assets and that enforced collection will cause a hardship you're possibly a good candidate for CNC status.

Typically, your account will be placed on hold for a year requiring you to submit updated financial information annually.

Keep in mind, CNC status does not stop penalties and interest from accruing. Therefore, if your financial condition improves, you will need to address your larger tax debt or face collection from the IRS again.

There is one very good point that you need to know about the CNC status. A CNC status does not stop the collection statute of limitations from running. Therefore, it is possible that the CSED will expire while you're in CNC status. If that happens, you will no longer owe the IRS for the tax debt.

If you believe that your financial condition will continue for a long time, it may make sense to just stay in CNC status until the CSED expires. However, if it will be temporary, it may be better to attempt an Offer in Compromise while your assets and income are low.

Although the penalties and interest continue to accrue while in CNC status, it's normally a small price to pay for immediate relief from aggressive collection activities. If you're struggling, make sure to ask your tax professional about this option.

Offer In Compromise

The Offer In Compromise program is the most well-known option for resolving a tax debt but it's also the most misunderstood and abused one. It seems like every radio, TV, or newspaper ad talk about settling your tax debt for "pennies on the dollar".

First, and foremost, this really does happen. The issue here is not the fact that it happens but that most people simply do not qualify. The big national firms use this promise all the time to attract and mislead desperate taxpayers.

Their process works like this. The big national firms will promise taxpayers a ridiculous settlement option and take a significant amount of money for the service. Once the IRS rejects the offer, the taxpayer is dropped and now owes more due to penalties & interest. In almost ALL cases, the client would never have qualified for the offer that was presented to the IRS. This common practice absolutely infuriates me and all I can do is help the taxpayer pick up the pieces and start over.

Hopefully, you will read this book and never fall victim to these despicable companies.

Now, the good stuff. In my opinion, the Offer In Compromise (OIC) program is a beautiful thing and if you are able to qualify, what an amazing way to get a fresh start.

An OIC is a written agreement between you and the IRS that settles your tax debt for less than what you actually owe. The program is a benefit to both the taxpayer and the IRS. The taxpayer gets to resolve an overwhelming tax debt and the IRS collects payments for taxes that it might not normally receive.

Like any other program, there have been ups and downs. The acceptance rate has often been very low. However, the IRS is trying to increase the offers accepted by making it easier to qualify. Based on recent statistics published by the IRS, the acceptance rate is currently over 40%.

I realize 40% doesn't sound very high but it is an improvement. In fact, I bet the acceptance rate would be much higher if the unscrupulous companies wouldn't submit offers that never had a chance of being accepted.

There are two types of offers, Doubt as to Liability and Doubt as to Collectability. Doubt as to Liability means just that, there is some reason to believe that you really don't owe the tax. The IRS is willing to settle the debt because they don't want to end up in litigation and have the tax court decide the outcome.

Although Doubt as to Liability is quite useful in the right circumstance, it is not nearly as common as the other, Doubt as to Collectability. Because of this, I'm only going to talk about Doubt as to Collectability.

Doubt as to Collectability

The most widely used form of OIC is the Doubt as to Collectability. The reasoning behind this program is that the IRS is most likely not going to collect more from you by using it's normal collections that it will receive by settling with you; hence the name "Doubt as to Collectability".

To qualify for an OIC, you must submit an offer that is acceptable to the IRS and meet certain requirements.

1) You MUST be current on ALL tax return filing.
2) You MUST make all current estimated tax payments for the year.
3) You MUST not be in bankruptcy.
4) You MUST agree to let the IRS keep any tax refunds that you are entitled to receive for the calendar year in which the offer is accepted by the IRS.

But, the burning question is, how much will it take to settle your debt? The answer is actually very complex and depends on several factors, including the amount of time needed to pay the offer, your assets, income, and expenses.

The amount that you MUST pay to the IRS is first determined by how long it will take you to pay the offer amount. There are currently two options: the "Lump Sum Cash" offer and the "Periodic Payment" offer.

Under the Lump Cash Offer, you must pay 20% of the total offer amount when the offer is submitted. In addition, you must pay the balance within 5 or fewer months of the date your offer is accepted. If you select this option, the IRS will require an offer that includes your "Remaining Monthly Income" X 12 months.

Under the Periodic Payment Offer, you must send the first payment when your offer is submitted, and then pay the remaining balance within the next 6 to 24 months based on the offer. If you select this option, the IRS will require an offer that includes your Remaining Monthly Income X 24 months.

But how much should you offer? There are four components that the IRS will normally consider in determining whether to accept your offer: your assets, your future income, the ability to collect from third parties, and assets beyond their reach.

The part of the calculation that is probably the most misunderstood of the entire process is probably your assets. The IRS will require an offer that includes the "net realizable equity" in your assets. The basic calculation for this is quick sale value (80% of Fair Market Value) less any amounts owed to secured lien holders that have priority over the IRS Tax Lien.

For example, I had a client who wanted to do an OIC but there was substantial equity in the home. Using the quick sale value and subtracting the mortgage amount still produced a figure that exceeded the total amount that was owed to the IRS. This meant he would never qualify for an OIC to resolve his tax problem. However, on more than one occasion he was advised to take this approach from other tax resolution companies, along with a significant fee.

Once the OIC is rejected, the next step is to spend additional money to either appeal or try an alternative. It doesn't matter because once they have your money and submit the OIC that is certain to be rejected, they have done their job.

So beware of tax resolution companies that are only suggesting an OIC. Of course, as a taxpayer, you have the right to apply for the program. However, why pay the money for something that you have zero chance of approval? You may as well throw your money in a burning barrel!

The IRS then considers your future income. Future income is the amount of money remaining after paying your qualified and allowable expenses.

This means that for most people, the expenses are understated which shows more money available to pay the IRS. Of course, this "available money" is only on paper. In most circumstances, there is no money left over or the IRS would have already been paid.

The calculation of your future income is very complex and requires the guidance of a tax resolution specialist. A tax resolution specialist will be able to analyze your situation and possibly find ways to maximize your expenses to lower the future income portion and lowering the amount of the offer.

Once your expenses have been maximized you must multiply the remaining monthly income by either 12 or 24, depending on the offer you are applying for. This total than gets added to the equity portion we discussed previously.

After the two most important pieces have been addressed, the ability to collect from third parties must be considered. This is the "look back period" and deals with the transfer of assets to someone else or maybe the assets are being held by someone else for your behalf. This isn't really an issue but on occasion it will be a problem if large assets are recently disposed of.

The last piece relates to assets that are beyond the reach of the IRS. These are assets that the IRS may not be able to levy or file a lien on. Perhaps these assets are in another country. The IRS can't file a lien in those countries. Even though the IRS is not able to file a lien or a levy you are required to disclose information about the assets.

Now that you have all of the pieces ready and have your reasonable offer calculated, it's time for the paperwork.

You will need a complete 433-A (OIC) if you are an individual and 433-B (OIC) if you own a business. You will need to provide extensive documentation for every number on the financial forms. The next step is to compete a Form 656 and send everything to the IRS along with an application fee. Don't forget the correct down payment amount will be dependent upon the offer you choose.

The OIC program is a wonderful program and has helped a lot of taxpayers get back on track. Just imagine, if your offer is accepted, you will be able to settle your tax debt for less than you owe. You can get your tax liens removed, improve your credit rating and stop worrying about the IRS once and for all.

However, you MUST be careful not to get swept away by the empty promises. Remember, if it sounds to good to be true, it probably is.

Innocent Spouse Relief

Another option is to blame your spouse or ex-spouse. This is called Innocent Spouse Relief and I personally think it is often overlooked as a viable option.

If you file a joint tax return with your spouse, each of you is jointly and severally liable for the entire tax debt. This means that the IRS can collect the entire tax debt from the two of you together or from each of you individually.

More often than not, it's the husband who is guilty of doing things to create the tax debt (sorry fellas). The wife signs the joint return, not understanding or completely unaware of her husband's financial situation. When the IRS begins sending the first of many collection notices, the result is often separation or even worse, divorce. This isn't always the scenario, it's just the most common one.

The IRS provides three types of relief to potentially escape the joint and several liability that you incurred with your spouse or ex-spouse.

1) Innocent spouse relief
2) Separation of liability relief
3) Equitable relief

Innocent Spouse Relief

The most common is the general rule for innocent spouse relief. However, the requesting spouse must meet ALL of the requirements.

1) A joint return was filed.
2) The tax reported on the return was understated.
3) You can prove that when you signed, you did not know and had no reason to know that the tax was understated.
4) Taking into account all of the facts and circumstances, it would be unfair hold the

requesting spouse liable for the understatement of tax.

5) You must seek innocent spouse relief within two years after the IRS begins collection activity.

The most difficult one to prove is #3, the innocent part of not knowing the tax was understated.

In determining whether the innocent spouse had reason to know, the IRS typically considers 6 factors.

1) The nature of what caused the understatement of tax.
2) The couples financial situation.
3) Your education background and business experience.
4) The extent of your participation in the activity that resulted in the understatement of tax.
5) Whether you inquired at, or before the time the return was filed, about items on the return.
6) Whether the underlying reason for the understatement represented a departure from a current pattern.

If you can prove that you didn't know and had no reason to know about the understatement you may qualify for innocent spouse relief. If you are currently married, consider filing married filing separately until your spouse resolves the tax issues.

Separation or Allocation of Liability Relief

The second form of relief from joint and several liability is separation or allocation of liability.

There are four conditions that must be met in order to qualify for this type of relief.

1) You filed a joint income tax return.
2) There is an understatement of tax that is solely attributable to the other spouse.
3) When you file for relief you are, no longer married to, legally separated from, or living apart for more than 12 months from the guilty spouse.
4) You seek relief within 2 years after the IRS begins collection activity.

This type of relief is often easier to receive than the standard innocent spouse relief. Keep in mind, the IRS will not apply the separate liability if you had actual knowledge of any item that caused the understatement. The IRS has the burden of proving that you had knowledge while with the standard innocent spouse option the burden of proof is on the requesting spouse.

There are a variety of additional rules and conditions regarding innocent spouse relief. This is only intended to give you a brief introduction of the available options.

Equitable Relief

The final option of innocent spouse relief is Equitable Relief. To qualify for Equitable Relief, you will need to meet certain requirements.

1) You are not eligible for innocent spouse or separation of liability relief.
2) You filed a joint tax return.

3) You seek innocent spouse relief within 2 years after the IRS begins collection activity.

4) You and your spouse did not transfer assets to one another as part of a scheme to defraud the IRS or third party creditors, former spouses or business partners.

5) Your spouse did not transfer property to you for the sole purpose of avoiding tax or the payment of tax.

6) You did not knowingly participate in the preparation and/or filing of a fraudulent tax return.

7) The tax debt is attributable, in full or in part, to an item of your spouse or former spouse or an unpaid tax resulting from their income. However, if the debt is partially yours, you can only get relief for the tax debt attributable to you spouse or former spouse. Hint: There may be ways that you can get around this rule, with the proper fact pattern.

Once you've met the conditions above, you will need to show that it would be unfair to hold you responsible for the debt and ask IRS to grant you equitable relief.

The IRS will consider the following in making their decision:

1) Marital status: Although it's not required If you're still married to your spouse, the IRS considers this factor neutral. However, the IRS will lean towards granting the relief if you are, no longer married to, legally separated, or living apart from the guilty spouse for more than 12 months.

2) Economic hardship: The IRS will consider granting relief if, by not doing so, it means that you won't be able to take care of your basic living

expenses. Point: remember the IRS' acceptable basic living expenses may not be the same as yours.

3) Knowledge: The IRS considers whether or not you had any way to know about the reporting issue. If you are able to demonstrate this, the IRS will strongly take this into consideration.

4) Legal obligation: The IRS also considers if there were legal obligations to pay the debt, such as due to a divorce decree. Just keep in mind, that tax law trumps family law.

5) Benefit, compliance, & health: The IRS will examine to see benefited from the unpaid tax debt. They will also review compliance since the incurring of the outstanding tax debt. Last, the IRS will also take into consideration your physical or mental health at the time the tax was incurred.

As you can see, the IRS has many factors to consider when granting equitable relief for some or even all of the tax debt.

If the circumstances are right, Innocent Spouse Relief can be a great option for resolving your tax debt.

Bankruptcy

I am only going to say this once; you can bankrupt out of taxes. However, not all taxes are dischargeable and certain criteria must be met. But as in all of the options I've provided, it is definitely worth considering in the right situation.

I am not an attorney so I can't offer a lot of information here. Your tax resolution specialist should carefully review your case to see if your particular situation would even qualify for bankruptcy.

Here are the basic rules when considering bankruptcy:

1) The debt must be income taxes;
2) The debt must have been due for at least 3 years, including extensions;
3) The debt must have been assessed for at least 240 days;
4) The tax return must have been filed at least 2 years;
5) The filed tax return cannot be fraudulent or an intent to willfully evade tax.

I always consider bankruptcy in my analysis and planning process. If it looks like a viable solution, I have a couple of bankruptcy attorneys that I will bring in on the case.

Unfortunately, I have worked with several individuals who filed bankruptcy only to find out the taxes were waiting for them on the other side. Or, even worse, if a little planning had been done the taxes would have been completely discharged. This literally breaks my heart. Not only do they have the rebuilding process from the bankruptcy, they still have to deal with their taxes.

Penalty abatement

Let's talk penalties! I often hear my clients complaining about all the penalties! If only the penalties were gone they could, sometimes even gladly, pay the taxes. However, it's a bit of a double edged sword. The penalties are there to discourage non-compliance. The penalties also make it difficult for a troubled taxpayer to get compliant. If there were no penalties, there would be no reason or incentive to file or pay on-time. Unfortunately, they are simply a necessary evil.

Fortunately, our tax code recognizes that sometimes the right thing to do is to reduce or completely eliminate the penalties.

In fact, many times I have been able to save my clients a significant amount of money by getting their penalties abated. However, beware of the resolution companies that advertise the very misleading concept of abating the penalties AND interest. Although it does happen, it's very rare. In fact, there are only 5 legitimate ways to get interest abated. Keep in mind, this does not apply to the interest that is automatically reduced when the penalties or tax debt is reduced. I'm only talking about interest in general.

> 1) The IRS assessed interest on tax that you didn't actually owe.

2) The IRS incorrectly issued a refund and is seeking repayment of the overpayment plus interest.

3) The interest is due to delays caused by the IRS in performing managerial acts.

4) The interest accrued more than 18 months after the tax was due or you filed the return, and the IRS failed to notify that additional tax was due.

5) The interest accrued on a tax return that you filed late because you were living in a federally declared disaster area when it was due.

That's it! As you can see, the criteria is very specific. Although it does happen, it is very unlikely. So if you hear of ANYONE offering to get your interest reduced or abated, just walk away.

Now that we have the bad news out of the way, let me share some good news. Penalty abatement is much more common. This option is underused for a variety of reasons. I assume the largest reason is a lack of understanding of our ridiculously complicated tax code. I often meet tax professionals and taxpayers who have no idea this is even allowed.

To make matters worse, a Governmental study of the penalty abatement usage found that in 63% of allowable cases a request was not made. Now I completely understand when a taxpayer does not utilize the penalty abatement option because they have no idea it's even possible. But, when the IRS employee or manager assigned to the case doesn't offer their assistance I personally think it is extremely abusive and should be against the law!

The various penalties that the IRS can assert is mind blowing. The most common penalties are: failure to file (FTF), failure to pay (FTP) and the penalty for not paying payroll taxes on-time. The failure to file penalty is 5% per month, up to a maximum of 5 months or 25%. The failure to pay penalty ranges from ¼% to 1%, up to a maximum of 25%. These penalties run simultaneously. Therefore, after two years 50% of your total tax bill could be penalties!

The penalty for not paying your payroll tax deposits start at 2% for 1-5 days late up to a maximum of 15% after being late for 10 days. This means that 62 ½% of a business tax bill may be penalties alone! Regardless of the penalty, it's easy to see how beneficial it can be to utilize the penalty abatement options.

Now the really good news! There are two options available: first time penalty abatement (FTA) or reasonable cause.

FTA is where the code actually gets it right. If you've been a good taxpayer, and have always filed and paid your taxes on time, you may be a very good candidate for the first time penalty abatement.

Individuals can request First Time Penalty Abatement for failure to file and failure to pay penalties. Businesses can request First Time Penalty Abatement for failure to file, failure to pay, and failure to deposit penalties.

As with anything else, the program does have certain criteria that must be met.

1) A Failure to File or Failure to Pay penalty has not been assessed in the three tax years prior to the year in question
2) You did not receive a First Time Penalty Abatement in the last three years.
3) All returns have been filed and either paid or arranged to be paid.

That's it! It's a wonderful program and can significantly reduce your overall tax debt. It also doesn't require any documentation or proof to support your request. In fact, it's almost a "gimme". But, you have to know it even exists because it's obvious the IRS isn't just giving it away.

But no worries! If you don't qualify for the First Time Penalty Abatement perhaps there was reasonable cause?

The Internal Revenue Manual lists many different "reasonable cause" arguments. These include:

1) You died or had a serious illness, or there was a death or illness of someone in your immediate family.
2) You had some type of unavoidable absence.
3) Your business was destroyed by fire, tornado or other casualty.
4) You were unable to determine the amount of deposit or tax due for reasons beyond your control.
5) Your ability to make tax deposits or payments was impaired by civil disturbances.
6) You didn't have the funds to pay the deposit or tax due. You must be able to demonstrate that

this happened even though you exercised ordinary business care and prudence.

7) You were unable to obtain necessary records.
8) A mistake was made.
9) You relied on erroneous advice, either from the IRS or from a third party.
10) You were ignorant of the tax laws.
11) You would have experienced an undue economic hardship if you had actually paid the tax.

To qualify for a penalty abatement based on reasonable cause, you must request the relief in writing, demonstrate that the event relates to the tax years involved, and SUPPORT your position with documentation.

I always review a situation to determine if they qualify for a first time penalty abatement. If not, I move on to the reasonable cause argument.

Make sure to ask your resolution specialist about penalty abatement (only if you're not using me because I obviously know about it ☺).

7. BUSINESS PROBLEMS

As a small business owner myself, I have a special appreciation for the drive and motivation that it takes to run a business. I also understand the unique problems that occur when trying to run a business and I understand how complicated the rules are.

There are several ways that business owners can get into trouble with the IRS. However, the two most common ways are not paying estimated tax payments and not paying payroll taxes. In fact, if I had to guess, I would say these two problems alone count for 80% of the overall total.

Estimated Tax Payment Problems

Our tax system is designed around a "pay as you earn" collection process. Therefore, if you are not receiving a paycheck with taxes being withheld, you are typically required to make estimated tax payments to the IRS. This means if you're a sole proprietor, partner, S corporation shareholder, and/or a self-employed individual, and you expect to report more than $1,000 on your tax return, you must pay estimated tax payments. These tax payments are required four times a year: April 15, June 15, September 15, & January 15.

The point of the estimated tax payment is to keep you on track with your income tax debt for the year. Ideally, if calculated correctly, there should not be any additional tax due at the end of the year. This is why most wage earners are usually not in trouble with the IRS.

Unless you are disciplined and pay your estimated tax payments as required, you may find yourself with a double whammy. April 15th rolls around, followed by October 15th when the extension runs out for last year's taxes. Even worse, you haven't paid any estimated taxes for the current year. It's easy to see how it can snowball and get out of control.

The reason that most self-employed business owners struggle with making estimated tax payments is usually because of cash flow. Usually the money barely comes in on a consistent enough basis to pay the employees, rent, or utilities. One way to keep things moving is by not paying the estimated tax payments.

I understand this because I deal with the same budgeting problems that my clients do. Therefore, if you haven't been able to pay your estimated tax payments and find yourself delinquent, you can use any of the techniques that we've discussed to address the debt.

Just remember that the IRS will require you to start making estimated tax payments and remain current going forward. So, most importantly….once you get current, do everything in your power to stay current!!!

Payroll Tax Problems

The next common problem with being self-employed – payroll taxes. However, problems with payroll taxes can quickly elevate to a much more serious level and can actually result in criminal charges.
If you have employees, each pay period you are required to withhold federal, state, Social Security and Medicare taxes.

You must then send these funds weekly, monthly or quarterly, depending on your requirements.

In essence, you are now a tax collector and entrusted with the duty of collecting and paying these to the government. You collect this money in "trust" for the government and you are liable for it until you turn it over to the government. The amount that you collect from your employees is called the "trust fund portion" of the payroll taxes.

Businesses must also pay to the government an amount for the employer's portion of the Social Security and Medicare tax. In general, a business must match the Social Security and Medicare contributions paid by the employees. This is known as the "non-trust fund portion" of the payroll taxes. These taxes are reported on form 941 for federal taxes.

Even though payroll taxes are required to be sent in weekly, monthly, or quarterly, the same cash flow problems that make estimated tax payments difficult will also impact the ability to make payroll tax payments.

So, when the rent is due and the employees need paid, small businesses and self-employed people take a short-term loan from the government. Rather than turning over the money collected from their employees for the payroll taxes, the business uses the money to fund operations, rent, and payroll.

The honest intention is that the money will be there next week and will be repaid. However, this can be a very expensive and dangerous approach!

Because, as we all know, life gets in the way and the money is than needed for something else. Before you know it, the payroll taxes are seriously delinquent and seem impossible to catch up.

Although not paying taxes is a problem, not paying payroll taxes especially the Trust Fund Portion of those taxes – is a REAL problem. The IRS - and the federal government – views your failure to pay the Trust Fund Portion as the theft. It was never your money, remember? You are merely the collector and holding the money in trust.

Don't expect much sympathy from the IRS in this situation. I frequently hear from taxpayers for the first time when the IRS wants to shut down their business for failing to pay payroll taxes. This is one area they are very serious about.

Fortunately, you can fix the payroll tax problems and still keep the business open using the techniques we've discussed. I've done this many times for my business clients.

Just as before, you must remain current going forward with your payroll tax payment requirements.

Unfortunately, sometimes it just isn't possible to keep the business operating. There isn't enough income to sustain the current operating expenses and catch-up the past-due bills.

When the business shuts down, the payroll tax debt is still an issue that must be dealt with. If your business was a sole proprietorship, partnership, or an LLC, the IRS can ultimately hold you personally responsible for the tax debt.

In this situation, many of the options we've previously discussed will be available. The IRS may also consider settling the debt with an Offer in Compromise without requiring you to pay the Trust Fund Portion of the tax debt.

However, if your business was a corporation, the IRS may instead assert the Trust Fund Recovery Penalty (TFRP) against you, personally. This is the portion of the payroll tax debt that was withheld from the employees. It's also called the 100% penalty because the IRS imposes 100% of this amount against a "responsible party".

But who can be a "responsible party"? As expected, most often the "responsible party" will be the owner or owners of the business but it doesn't always stop there.

The IRS may also try to impose the TFRP against employees, contractors, spouses, and so forth. Just like a law suit, they'll throw everyone in the tank and pull them out one by one for a determination.

Therefore, if you're in a position that any of the following criteria may apply, listen up!

1) Are you collecting or paying withheld payroll or excise taxes?
2) Have you intentionally not collected or paid these funds over?
3) Have you paid other creditors instead of the Government?

Although the IRS will usually consider anyone with check signing authority as a "responsible party", this should not be the sole factor or criteria when making the determination. However, that doesn't usually stop them from trying!

In order to determine who is responsible, the IRS will begin by interviewing their "suspects". I would recommend that you have a professional around for this. The interviewing process can be very confusing, overwhelming, and self-incriminating.

Ultimately, it is in your best interest to be fully aware of the consequences of your actions when handling or managing payroll taxes.

I completely understand how self-employed and small business owners end up in trouble. It is incredibly difficult to draw that line in the sand knowing that when you reach it, everything changes.

Most importantly, if you are delinquent, you must find a way to become current or eventually the IRS can, and will, shut you down!

Sometimes it makes sense to work with a payroll service that handles all of your payroll tax withholdings, deposits, and reporting. I like to think of it as a form of "forced" cash flow management. For some business owners, it forces them to live within their budget.

Most importantly, if you are in trouble with the IRS, I urge you to find a tax resolution specialist. In the most critical situation, they may be the only thing standing between enforced IRS collection procedures and keeping the doors open.

With a little bit of creativity and planning, a variety of solutions may be available. However, these are very specialized services and can be costly. The benefit of using a tax resolution specialist most often exceeds the cost, especially in some of the most complicated and expensive cases!

8. THE DREADED AUDIT

There are few things in our nation that everyone will agree on, but the dread or fear of an IRS audit may be at the very top of the list.

Unfortunately, there are multiple reasons for this fear, some are realistic and some are not. In fact, this fear is the main reason the IRS scammers have been so lucrative and successful. People are literally terrified of the IRS, and rightly so.

Fortunately for you, after this chapter, you should have a basic understanding of the audit process and what to expect.

The IRS generally has three years, after a tax return has been filed, to select it audit. This filing date can be a bit tricky but if you file before the due date, the return is considered filed as of the due date, typically April 15th or October 15th for individuals.

Unfortunately, if the income on the tax return was understated by 25% or more, the IRS has six years to audit the return. If you file a fraudulent return, it's even worse! There is no time limit for the IRS to audit a fraudulent return. So, don't EVER file a fraudulent return and always file on time!

There is a bit of good news in all of this. The likelihood of an audit is actually relatively rare. Approximately 1% or less of all returns filed are ever selected for audit.

What you may find really surprising is that reporting NO income will generate a higher chance of being audited than someone reporting $500,000 in income.

Another factor that will significantly increase the risk of audit is being self-employed. The largest division within the IRS is the Small Business/Self-Employed Division – and they handle the most number of audits. The IRS believes that self-employed business owners are more likely to under-report income and overstate expense than regular W-2 wage earners. Unfortunately, they are correct.

As with any industry, the IRS is relying on computers and software more each and every day. They have developed a computer program called the Discriminant Inventory Function System (DIF) which assigns a numeric score to each tax return. The exact formula is secret, however, we believe that one of the areas being analyzed is the ratio of deductions to income.

If your ratio of deductions to income is too high, compared to the "norm" for your industry, you'll be assigned a high DIF number. This creates a greater opportunity to receive an audit notice.

The IRS also utilizes a second program called the Unreported Income Discriminant Index Formula (UIDIF). This program searches for tax returns that show high expenses and low income. This allows the IRS to look for taxpayers who under-report their income by examining expenses that seem high relative to the reported income.

In addition, the IRS uses another program called the Information Returns Processing System (IRP). This is what tax professionals refer to as the "matching program". The IRP system compares the data it receives from employers, banks, social security administration, & other business entities such as partnerships & corporations to items reported on your tax return. If there is a discrepancy, you will receive a notice.

Now that we have a really brief inside look on the selection process, I want you to be aware of the types of audits. However, one thing to note, the local IRS field office will make the final determination on who actually gets audited. Once they have made a determination, the audit may be conducted in one of three ways: correspondence, office, and field.

Correspondence Audit

A correspondence audit is the most common type of audit. More than 75% of all audits are done by mail. The IRS uses this method to verify information with records that you can easily send to the IRS in the mail.

If you receive a correspondence audit notice, you and your tax professional will want to respond quickly and within the time specified in the notice. By the way, as bad as it feels, be thankful it's not an in-person audit!

Office Audit

The next form of audit is the Office Audit. You will normally receive a notice from the IRS that sets an appointment date and time. It may also request that you call the IRS office for an appointment. The notice will most likely request that you bring specific documentation and the areas that the IRS plans to examine.

These audits are conducted at the local IRS office, typically only focusing on the specific items listed in the notice. The audit should not focus on everything listed on the return, just those specific items.

If you are working with a tax professional, you won't ever need to meet with the IRS auditor. Your tax professional can attend on your behalf and take care of the entire thing.

Field Audit

The last form of audit is, by far, the worst form because it is the most intrusive. The IRS typically uses its most experienced auditors to conduct field examinations. The idea of a field audit is that they conduct the audit in your home or place of business, usually wherever the books and records are maintained.

You should keep the auditor away from your home or business, even if you have nothing to hide. Unfortunately, my experience is that you are guilty until proven innocent. By visiting your home or office, the auditor may get an impression that you have more income than reported, based solely on the physical environment using it for a lifestyle assessment.

The Taxpayer Bill of Rights allows you to refuse the audit on your business premises if it would have a negative impact on your business. You may want to request the audit be held at the local IRS office instead.

I would strongly encourage you to hire a tax professional to represent you. Your tax professional can insist that the audit be conducted at the tax professional's office, rather than your own.

The Process

Regardless of the form of audit, the audit will typically only focus on specific issues related to the tax return. The auditor cannot ask questions that don't specifically relate to the return selected for audit. They will still ask the questions, but you have the right to decline.

At the end of the audit, the auditor will hand or mail an Examination Report-Form 4549. There are two possible outcomes of the audit. First, the report says there are "no changes" to your return. That is a very best kind of report!

However, more likely than not, the report will list proposed changes (additions or deletions) to your tax return. In addition, they will include the interest and possible penalties. If you agree with the proposed changes, you must sign the Form 4549 and return it with a Form 870-Consent to Proposed Tax Adjustment. The IRS calls this an agreed case.

If you disagree with the proposed changes, you can request clarification from the auditor or the opportunity to provide additional documentation. You can also request another meeting with the auditor or even meet with the auditor's manager.

If you continue to disagree, there reaches a point where the IRS will send you a 30-day letter. This is the formal notice to you that it considers your case "unagreed" and that you have 30 days to appeal the audit. If you file an appeal within the 30-day time period, your case will be moved to the Appeals Office.

If you don't file the request to appeal, the case will be closed and the IRS will send you a 90-day letter (Notice of Deficiency). At this point, you will need to file a petition in the U.S. Tax Court within 90 days or the report will become final. Unfortunately, this means you will lose any right to contest the audit.

Any time a return is selected for audit, there is a significant risk for substantial tax increases. The tax increase will determine the interest and any penalties that may be applied. Therefore, I would strongly recommend you do NOT try to handle this yourself. The stress and frustration alone can make working with a tax professional extremely worthwhile. When you throw in the potential tax savings and never having to meet with the IRS directly, I believe the benefits will outweigh the costs.

CONCLUSION

Whether your problem is big or small, really doesn't matter because neither one will simply go away and both are guaranteed to grow! I know your problem seems intimidating and overwhelming, but you are not alone. We are here now, tomorrow, and whenever you need us. You just need to be ready to step aside and let us take over because we got this! I, along with my team of professionals, take a limited number of new tax resolution cases each month to ensure that we can give each case the time and attention needed to achieve the best outcome and resolution possible. When you are ready to start living and enjoying life, call us, toll free at 1-844-TAX-MESS (1-844-829-6377)

ABOUT THE AUTHOR

Alissa is a CPA & Certified Tax Resolution Specialist (CTRS) in Arkansas. She lives with her crazy, fun loving husband, and a grumpy, little dog named Tater Bug. Although there are 3 children, they are all out of the house, except for when they come home (duh, huh?) She has practiced accounting for 16 years, with a sincere passion for fair and effective tax administration.